T0288628

I Never Dared Hope for You

.

I NEVER DARED HOPE FOR YOU

(lyric essays)

by Christian Bobin

translated from the French by Alison Anderson

AB

Autumn Hill Books

Iowa City, Iowa

CONTENTS

This is an Autumn Hill Books Book
Published by Autumn Hill Books, Inc.
P.O. Box 22
Iowa City, Iowa 52244

Printed in the United States of America

First published as *L'inespérée*
© 1994 Editions GALLIMARD, Paris

Cet ouvrage, publié dans le cadre d'un programme d'aide à la
publication, bénéficie du soutien du Ministère des Affaires étrangères et
du Service Culturel de l'Ambassade de France aux Etats-Unis.

This work, published as part of a program of aid for publication, received
support from the French Ministry of Foreign Affairs and the Cultural
Services of the French Embassy in the United States.

Autumn Hill Books ISBN-13: 978-0-9754444-9-8
Library of Congress Control Number: 2009929410

http://www.autumnhillbooks.org

A letter to the light that lingered
in the streets of Le Creusot, in France,
on Wednesday, December 16, 1992,
at around two o'clock in the afternoon

Madam,

I first noticed you only at the beginning of the after-
noon, and — forgive the paltriness of this confes-
sion — that was no doubt because I had nothing better
to do, as I was waiting outside a music school where
children were going in, loaded down with instruments
sometimes bigger than they were.

You were there long before I was. You had arrived that
day from the depths of time in order to take your first
and last steps on earth. As I'm not a morning person, I
did not have the joy of knowing you when you were

young. The woman I saw crossing a sky paralyzed with cold was already mature, somewhat weary from hours of wandering, but she was, without any doubt whatsoever, the most beautiful woman I had ever met. Beauty, madam, has no other heart than yours. I looked at you in the way a lover or a painter might have. Atoms dancing in the void and the terrifying patience of God had dressed you in a fairy's gown. I looked at you as if I were someone who had nothing left to do with his life—only live it with as much secret joy, in as carefree a manner, as possible.

You were going everywhere at once, like a laughing child. You were the image of a life detached from the self, generous to itself and perfectly nonchalant with regard to the days to come. While the children were having their music lesson, I was having a lesson in goodness from you: it is in your image that I would like to go into the handful of days given to me, madam; with your joyfulness and carefree love of losing yourself.

We are all searching for just one thing in life: to find fulfillment, to receive a kiss of light on our gray hearts, to know the sweetness of a love that will not fade. To be alive is to be seen, to step into the light of a loving gaze: no one escapes this law, not even God who, in principle, because he is supposed to be the principle behind everything, is outside the law. The Bible is nothing but the inventory of God's extravagant efforts to be seen by us, if only for an instant, if only by one man and even if that man is a good-for-nothing or a goatherd stupefied by solitude and bad wine. It's all there. God makes use of whatever means he can to draw our attention to him, from the heavy machinery of floods and storms with their tin-can clatter, to the scarcely audible whimpering of a newborn babe lying in the straw, lulled by the labored breathing of an ass and an ox. This last attempt is of course what worked: you can only see when not a single shadow of power remains. Power makes one blind, glory casts a gloom. In days of old, princes would come out of their palaces in grand array: carriages, horses, valets, banners, processions of all kinds. The word disarray comes from this. To be in disarray is to be deprived of an escort, to move into a life stripped of any sort of protective cloak of force. God in his adornments of lightning or royalty is insignificant. God in the sleep of a newborn child or the disarray of your bearing—that is immense, madam, immense.

I know people who would make you smile and, most likely, you would not manage to dazzle them, withdrawn as they are in the sorrows of their libraries or their laboratories. These people diligently research the depth of things, the final explanation of the world. In their meditative mania they overlook nothing but one detail: no one can keep the truth close to himself, even in the prison of a formula. Truth is not something one can have, only live. Truth is you, madam: from the light that comes, the light that goes. The deepest mystery is revealed in you, given to those who wish for it.

I must make a confession: for a long time I did not love you. For a long time I did not love your sisters. A sky released from shadow was horrifying to me. I cared only for gray weather, and that was because of the melancholy inside me, the insect of melancholy crawling through me as if through a hollow, worm-eaten tree stump. It is an illness that affects the spirit with a certainty all the greater for one's fear of losing it: the melancholic person is convinced he has lost everything—except his melancholy, to which he clings fiercely. It is the affliction of those who, disappointed that they are not everything, choose, in a childish reversal of pride, to become nothing, keeping only those things in the world that resemble them: the dreary, the rainy. I've recovered from that affliction, madam. I am not sure how, but it's all over now. Today I know how to love you, and if I still have a taste for gray skies, it is calmer: I like them because they are, not because they confirm some catastrophe experienced in my mind.

Basically, even in the midst of one of my attacks of melancholy, I was never too sure what to do with this life except love it, love it to distraction and tell it so: write love letters, illuminate the whiteness of a sheet of paper by sprinkling ink on it. It would seem that, in the long run, this has become my main occupation: a small craftsman's trade, not unlike painting icons. Here with ink, there with gold, the same slowness is required, the same invisible thing brought forth to be seen. I love you, madam—even if this love is not and never will be the equivalent of an acknowledgment to the world: one cannot feel the sweetness of this life without at the same time feeling an absolute rage against the evil that presses it from all sides. This is a rule obeyed by painters when they intensify their dark colors so that the light ones will be truly light.

The composition of love letters is, to be sure, not a very serious occupation and lacks great economic importance. But if no one practiced it anymore, if no one reminded life of its own purity, then life would end up letting itself wither away and die, don't you think?

These are some of the thoughts you've given me while I watched you carry this day toward the coming winter, holding it in your naked arms like a bouquet of fresh flowers. And suddenly I understood that you would not come back into my life, that I would die without ever seeing you again: tomorrow, one of your sisters might descend from the sky to light our way in our dreary occupation, but never again will it be you.

How can I put it more simply: I shall love your sisters with the same love, for I have a changing heart, out of loyalty to the mere passage of life through my life. But I cannot abandon you to the void without recalling your name and thanking you for this visit that has ended with your defeat: at five o'clock in the afternoon, in the middle of December, the shadows have reclaimed their rights.

A few stars were approaching and in their brightness I glimpsed a fragment of your vanished soul—cheerful and frivolous, unforgettable.

2

She is dirty. Even clean she is dirty. She is covered in gold and excrement, in children and saucepans. She is omnipotent. She is like a greasy, dirty queen who has nothing left to govern, as she has already invaded everywhere, has already contaminated everything with her intrinsic filth. No one can resist her. She reigns by virtue of an eternal yearning for the depths, for the black hole of time. In prison she is like a tranquilizer. In certain psychiatric hospital wards she is always on duty. It is in such places that she is most in her element: no one looks at her, no one listens to her, they let her waffle on in her corner, they place before her those they no longer know what to do with. A day in a hospital or a prison is longer than a day. You have to get through it. They have her look after the mental patients, the prisoners and the old men in retirement homes. She has infinitely less dignity than those people, knocked senseless by age, wounded by Law or by nature. She could not care less about this so-called dignity she lacks. She does her work and that is enough. Her work is to soil the pain with which she has been entrusted, and to amass everything—childhood and misfortune, beauty and laughter, intelligence and money—into a single slimy glazed block. Commonly referred to as a window on the world. But, more than a window, it's the entire world crammed into that block, the world bathed in that light of hers, lousy with people, with the world's rubbish spilled, every second of the day, onto the living room carpet. Of course you can always rummage around. Sometimes, particularly in the early hours of the morning, you happen upon new words, fresh faces. You might discover a treasure in the trash dump. But there's no point in sorting through it, the garbage cans come too quickly, the handlers too fast on their feet. You feel sorry for those people. You feel sorry for television reporters, with their perfect lack of intelligence and heart — that affliction with time they have, inherited from the business world: tell me about God and about your mother, you have one minute and twenty-seven seconds to answer my question. A friend of yours, a philosopher, spends a day there, inside that window soiled with images. They ask him to come to speak about love, and because they are afraid of a word that might take its time, afraid something might happen, because whatever the cost nothing un-ambiguous or depressing must be allowed to happen — that is, *less than nothing* — because of this fear of theirs, they invite twenty other people, specialists in this, experts in that, twenty people; in other words, three minutes per person. Children are told that vulgarity is found in words. True vulgarity in this world is found in time, in the inability to spend it in any other way than as if it were money, hurry, hurry from a catastrophe to the horse racing results, hurry to glide across tons of money and a deep lack of intelligence about life, what life is in its suffering magic, hurry on to the next hour and above all don't let anything happen, any true word, any pure astonishment. And your friend, after the program, he's a bit concerned all the same, why such a hatred of thought, such a mania for chopping everything up, and the producer gives him this magnificent reply: I agree with you, but it's better that I'm here, if others were in my place, it would be even worse. Her answer makes you think of certain officials of the French state during World War II, of the legitimacy that these virtuous civil servants of evil conferred upon themselves: it was necessary to take charge of deporting France's Jews, that allowed us to save a few of them. The same abject behavior, the same collaboration with the forces in the world that ruin the world, the same utter lack of common sense: there are seats one must leave empty. There are acts one cannot commit without immediately being undone by them. Television, despite its claims to the contrary, gives no news of the world. Television is the world collapsing onto the world, a whining drunken brute, incapable of offering a single clear, comprehensible piece of news. Television is the world working full time, filled to the brim with suffering, it's impossible to watch it under such conditions, impossible to hear. You sit there in your armchair or in front of your plate, and they toss a corpse at you followed by a soccer goal, and they leave you there together, the three of you, the dead man's nakedness, the soccer player's laughter, and your own life, already dark enough, they leave each of you at opposite ends of the earth, far apart because you were so brutally brought together—a dead man still dying, a soccer player still raising his arms, and you still struggling to make sense of it all, but they are off to something else, low pressure zone over Brittany, calm weather in Corsica. And so. And so what are you supposed to do with the old queen, stuffed full of images, dead drunk with money? Nothing. You mustn't do anything. There she is, crazier and crazier, sick at the idea that one day she may no longer be able to seduce. There she is and she won't budge. A world without images has become unthinkable. There will always be enterprising young people to serve her, to do her dirty work in your place, in the place of all, in the name of all. You have to let such baseness continue to abase itself, let the organic decomposition of the world proceed. It's near the end already, the end is nigh, one mustn't interrupt the death watch, or above all attempt to repair what has gone wrong—you might as well try to put foundation make-up onto the waxy cheeks of a dead woman. Let the blind images proliferate: something is coming up from below, something is coming to greet us. In pain there is an inexhaustible purity, the same that's found in joy, and this purity is making its way beneath the tons of the frozen imaginary. In the meanwhile, the true images, the pure images of truth take refuge in writing, in the solitary compassion of those who write, Velibor Čolić, for example. A Yugoslav writer, his images are not beautiful, he tells what he sees, it's as simple as that. He tells the story of something that happens in Modriča, in Bosnia-Herzegovina, on May 17, 1992. He tells this story as if it were an eternal thing. In the singularity of a place and an act he sees what has been eternal about the world since its worldly beginnings: and so you can read without losing courage, without saying to yourself, what's the use; and so you can give to the sentence the time to be written, and to the pain of the world the time to enter your mind and deliver its meaning there. You read: *The gypsy Ibro earned his living by re-selling old newspapers and empty bottles. He was the owner of a tumble-down cart, and several generations of the inhabitants of Modriča had heard his famous cry, early in the morning: "Transportation of every kind! Dead or alive, same price!" He lived in a strange cottage, on a street near the Medical Clinic. He had a wife who was a deaf-mute and a son who was fifteen or so, a mental retard. On*

*May 17, when the Serb army thrust its way into Mo-
driča, the gypsy Ibro refused to flee, even though he
was a Muslim. There was no pity for him. The Serb
soldiers slit his throat, and that of his wife and son and,
as in the "time of the Turks," they impaled their heads
on the stakes of the fence around the house. According
to eyewitnesses, on the table in the courtyard there
stood a bottle of raki and some freshly-made coffee. To
greet the soldiers if they came.* You read this and you
see Ibro and his wife and son, and the child-like cheer-
fulness of the murderers, the heads on the stakes and
the fresh coffee. The television might have shown you
the coffee but it would have insisted on the heads,
muttering something like, "We hesitate to show you
this," and on with the rest of the news, we haven't got
all day, low pressure zone over Corsica, calm weather
in Brittany. And you would have sat on in your dining
room, stupid, three heads on the table. There you have
all of it—and the tragic purity of all of it: the hospital-
ity granted to assassins. The evil of television is not in
television itself, it is in the world, and if we confuse the
two, it is because television and the world now com-
prise one lost and suffering mass. The evil in the world
has always been there, in the refusal of hospitality—the

first sacred fire of human history, before even God emerged. It is the world's evil, and it is what both the world and the image-sated monster suffer from: failure to welcome the weak images of pain, to recognize the basic laws of hospitality, which state that one gives water to anyone who comes from so far away. I entertain, says the television, yet it has been a long time since it has made us laugh. One can't provide culture for everyone, says the television, and we don't dare reply that it is not a problem of culture but of intelligence, which is not in the same category at all. Intelligence has nothing to do with diplomas. They can go together but diplomas are not the main ingredient. Intelligence is the solitary strength of finding, in the chaos of one's life, a gleam of light powerful enough to light the way a little beyond oneself—toward that next person, over there, lost like us in the dark. I have a soft spot for feelings, says television, and no one has the courage to point out the abyss between feelings and sentimentality. At the end of its tether, television says, it's not me, it's people, I just do what people want—and what response other than silence can you give when you're confronted with the grave illiteracy of television and of those who make it. The word people is one of the finest words in the language. In French it speaks of want and stubbornness, the nobility of the beggars beneath the careless heel of the nobles. It says the very opposite of what television says. And for the time being that's the way things stand: pain arrives famished in television's arms, only to be shunted into your own arms still unfed, only seen and heard. Then it sets off again, to seek asylum in ink, until the day comes when it can return to the temple of images — because one thing is absolutely certain: one day there will be someone intelligent enough to film a bottle of raki and freshly-made coffee, and they will take their time, they will say what they think is right, or keep silent, because sometimes it is necessary to keep silent in order to say what is right — and to show, however long it takes, simply show, with great calm, a bottle of raki and freshly-made coffee.

Passing Through Images

3

You arrive at his place in late afternoon. His place in Haute-Savoie. His house, his farm, his hideaway of ink and wood. You arrive there the way you arrive everywhere, impatient to get going again soon. It's an affliction you have, you cannot imagine a voyage as anything other than a detour on your way from your place back to your place. Very quickly, wherever you happen to be, even among the people you love, you succumb to the languor of the walls and windows of your solitude. Sleep is what you need, the drowsiness that overcomes you for hours on end in your apartment, while you do nothing, read nothing, write nothing, and you can't expect to go to other people's homes and then just disappear so you can rest your eyes, your speech, your soul, you can't ask those you love to put up with such a feeble, almost vanishing presence. It's stronger than you: you have to turn down a considerable number of invitations just to preserve a thing that is best described by the word "nothing": doing nothing, saying nothing, almost being nothing. It's where you discover the subtle heart of time, pumped by the nothing of blood in your veins. It's a border state that is vital to you, a thin line of nothing between boredom and despair — and joy walks a tightrope along that line, a joy fed precisely by nothing, by a glance at the day's sky, for example, from the bed where you lie, an active invalid doing nothing in your far niente of writing: a transparent light. A blue without density. It is as if the angels had just done their laundry and, owning no other wealth than love, they are always clothed in the same light, worn transparent from so many washings. In such blue beauty you sense the darkness into which the light will soon fall, and in this conjugal life of blue and black you find the one lesson of things that suits you, the proof of a certain excellence in this life where everything is given to us, every instant, blue with black, strength with hurt. There is only one sadness you might encounter there: how to receive life and yet not darken it with the feeling that something is owed to you. Nothing is owed to us in life, not even the innocence of a blue sky. Great art is the art of thankfulness for the abundance of every moment. Writing is a Chinese variant of this thankfulness, a curtsey to life in its cloak of nothing, lined with love. Yes, but the problem remains: who or what to thank? Who or what is behind the blue and black curtain? This is something you've never known. You've never known to whom your scribbled sentences might be addressed, the ink dabbed like perfume upon the flesh of white paper. That is why you are on your way to Haute Savoie, to talk about that with this writer you love, though you've never met him. And of course things don't turn out the way you expected. You go into the house and to begin with you don't see him, you see her, his companion, with her back to the window where a bit of sky is blazing. She stands at the ironing board. The sky, the ironing board, the laundry, her hands, her face: you look at this picture, you wonder why it has immediately parted from the colors you first saw, as if it were covered by a fine golden film. Initially you identify the sorry male dream of a housebound woman rooted to her home in the service of her family. Yes, initially there is — you cannot hide the thought — the very male fascination with a woman who might be what no other woman ever is: as perfect as a picture. That is how men must perceive their wives as they watch them ironing: at that particular moment, they are convinced that their woman will not leave them, as if the ephemeral nature of what that woman is doing will ensure the eternal nature of her presence. There will always be ironing to be done; therefore she who does it will always be there. There are other glimmers in this image: ironing is a chore; therefore it is tedious, but the sleepwalking element of each gesture allows the woman who is doing it to enter a slightly meditative state. Husbands are wrong to be so easily reassured: the woman who is ironing is also at that very moment at the far side of the planet, in the uninterrupted fugue of her heart. There is also the delicate nature of the things her hands are touching: cotton, wool, silk. Clothing is the body's ultimate armor. The woman who cares for clothes, who washes them and renews them with the heat of the iron is like a woman exploring the secrets of the flesh with a gentle, calming touch. And now, since silliness and intelligence are on such intimate terms in your head, you burst out laughing, though your face is implacable, as you say to yourself: that's enough. You already have a tendency to view mothers as saints, you're not going to start celebrating the docile spouse nailed to her ironing board for eternity, stop right there, I beg you, stop. Long after this flow of adoration and stupidity, what remains is the proof you have been given of peace, unwittingly bestowed by women who believe that they are doing no more than tend to everyday life, never suspecting the nobility of their tending nature. And now you see him and turn to greet him — a writer. What are they like, writers, in your mind: it may seem strange, but initially it's not about writing. A writer is someone who struggles with the angels of solitude and truth. A confused struggle, without any clear conclusion. A street fight, gangs brawling, feathers flying every which way and sometimes, as with every confrontation, a moment of peace. A book from time to time. But not always, not necessarily. You've actually met people who were overwhelmed by their own words. Their conversation radiated a true intelligence, not a conventional one, but when those people took up writing, it all vanished: as if the fear of writing poorly and the belief that there are rules caused them all of a sudden to lose all personal truth. Those are the people you recognize as true writers. It's not ink that makes writing, but a voice, the solitary truth of the voice, the hemorrhaging of truth into the guts of the voice. A writer is anyone who follows only the truth of who they are, without ever relying on anything other than the poverty and solitude of that truth. In this respect, children and women in love are born writers. One day you held in your hands a flower of a book title, the title alone: *The Afternoon of a Writer*. Before you even became acquainted with the story, it seemed obvious that it would show you a writer in the hours when he is not writing. The first word—afternoon—thus destroyed the second—writer. The story came to mind on the basis of the cover alone: the afternoon was there before the writer, and an absolute mystery emerged from their encounter: how does this person who writes spend his time when he is not writing? The answer—in your head, not in the book—was as follows: he goes on writing. Not with words, not with ink. But he is always writing. And then the following question had to be asked: what sort of writing is it that has no need of words to exist? Or even: someone who does nothing—what does he do? This is a question that interests you to the highest degree, for which you'll never find an answer, no doubt, not even here in Haute-Savoie. The man opposite you is like his books: gnarled and tender. He is in life as he is in his books—with the exception, perhaps, of one image. This nothing of an image that he shares with you, too light to insert in his books, too crazy to remain dormant: the image of his mother fleeing from the family home, fleeing from the ironing board, to run across a London bridge, his young and poorly educated mother running like a hunted animal through the streets of London, arriving breathless in a museum to look at a painting, one single painting by Turner: a sky smudged with light, a square of silence. You discover more about him in this image than in his books. It's as if he were saying to you: I am the child of a woman whose heart is the color of the sky, it is a mother's madness that gives birth to the madness of writing. And the hours go by. Afternoon, evening, night. The next day he walks you back to your car and just before he closes the car door he gives you this second image: "One day I was at the Abbey of Hautecombe, not far from here. I'm not a believer. I'm a communist. It's not the same thing—but it's just as impoverished, just as lost. Communist or believer—two words nobody knows how to use anymore.

They've been dragged through the mud, and someday they'll come back like new. Someday someone will have the utterly simple idea of exposing them to the light of his mind, of cleansing them with a rush of fresh thought, and then we'll realize how much we've missed those words, how well they know us, by heart. I went to the abbey because I have a friend there. I saw him, I said goodbye, then I lingered on a bench in the chapel. It was at the end of the day. I didn't hear them closing the doors: suddenly I was sitting there in the dark. There was only one source of light: an icon that no doubt stays lit day and night, gold on the face of a sixteen-year-old mother. It is the mother of Christ. There's no more merit in being the mother of Christ than in being the mother of any child: a mother's work is always impossible, and yet somehow she manages. It's incredible, a thing like this, incredible. And while sitting there in the dark I observed the beauty of this sixteen-year-old child, as pregnant, so to speak, as can be —yes, it's fair to say it as trivially as that: a woman who is with child, whether that child is Jesus Christ or an assassin, has eyes blazing with sweetness and fear in her irises —and while I was gazing at her I heard a buzzing sound, and this buzzing sound became a murmur, and the murmur became a flow, a tide of low, male voices, harmonizing: the monks had just come in for one of their ritual prayers. A herd of deep voices, an army of heavy men who had come to stand at the feet of a sixteen-year old girl illuminated with joy and pain. So you see, what lies at the depths of their words of praise, what is found at the extreme end of the gesture of those who receive and bow down as they do may be no more than that: a face, lost in the way a child's is, a face so frightened that words might make her run away—unless they are chanted in love, a nocturnal chant, blue with the voices of lovers." On your way home, with the speed of the car, the icons of the woman ironing and of the pregnant adolescent come together and exchange their colors and curves, then disappear gradually. There you are again at home by the open window, doing nothing, not even writing, not even seeing the saint in her gilded cage or the servant in her blue sky—seeing only a lost woman on every bridge in London, neither mother nor wife, just a woman crossing the skies, in passionate pursuit of a question indifferent to its answer: what love is it, then, that has no need of words to call to us? In whose image are we made, to take such delight in a simple image, a square of light on a dark wall?

Tea without Tea

4

The words are behind a table, on a podium. You are seated with the others at your desk in the auditorium and the words rise toward you, the fragrance of scholarly words, scrolls of the gray words. Five hundred adults, many women, many bent over their desks, writing, taking notes that they will not reread, and their expressions are filled with seriousness, the seriousness of those striving to hear well, the way one strives to eat well, without spilling anything next to one's plate, the seriousness of obedient children, preoccupied with learning well in order to get a good grade and be worthy of the teacher's love. Five hundred children between the ages of thirty and fifty, with the weakness of those who know nothing and to whom all shall be revealed. You've been to this sort of gathering, where words are behind the table. In the most varied locations, be it industry or the university. And there is always a similar joyfulness on most of the faces, and boredom on yours, the wise word metamorphoses into a headache the moment it reaches you, from the opening phrases of the lecture, the lesson, or the seminar. For a long time you could not avoid this sort of punishment, it was part of your work. That work went on for ten years and several times a year you had an appointment with the headache-inducing word. Two or three days at a round table, observing the sky through the window — a sky that was never as beautiful as during those hours of penitence. Only once were you able to desert. You invented a pretext and spent two delightful days, far away, so far from the scholarly words, the illiterate voices. On that day some children had invited you to play with them, to come to a dolls' tea party. Squeezing into a tiny cabin of corrugated metal all the way at the end of the garden, they invited you to share tea without water, tea without tea, a nonexistent tea, poured into dirty plastic cups. You accepted their invitation, and slowly you sipped the invisible tea, and as you tasted it you commented on it, while only a few hundred meters away the conference was slipping deeper and deeper into deadly boredom—a repast of shadows around a table of shadows. Your work gave you boredom with money. When after ten years it came to an end it took away the money—and the boredom. You have not attended any conferences since then. Sometimes someone says to you, what a pity. The people around you find it quite interesting to spend a certain number of hours without moving amid the darkness of a word. Whatever it was that gave you the incredible headaches was always very interesting, very instructive to them. Engineers at seminars, teachers in training, sociologists at conferences—they're all glad to be there. They spend two, even three days there. They don't go home, they listen to interesting things and it's a change from everyday life. Perhaps that is what you find so hard to bear. That's all it is: a change from everyday life. Because there's nothing you know better than the everyday nature of the life you are in, there's nothing you prefer to the taste of your ordinary solitude in this silent life, far from the marble of words, the tombs of faces. Life in society is when everyone is there and no one is present. Life in

31

society is when everyone obeys what no one wants. Writing is a way of escaping this impoverishment, a variation on solitude like love or gambling—a principle of insubordination, a virtue of childhood. So why are you there today? You are in that auditorium partly for the sake of money, partly for the sake of friendship. You've been invited to read some texts at the end of the evening. You'll be paid for your reading. The person who invited you is a psychiatrist. He is presiding over the conference but you don't consider him an authority, he's more like a child. A malicious child of fifty, concerned by what he sees, laughing at what he thinks. And how can you refuse an invitation from a child? But neither money nor friendship alone would have sufficed: curiosity swayed your decision and brought you here, to an auditorium at the medical school. Teachers, business leaders, writers—you're somewhat familiar with them. You know what each of them is like when they are alone, and what they turn into when they are put together in an auditorium. But you know nothing about psychiatrists, except that they touch death with the fingers of one hand and life with the other, and you are curious to see how one can accommodate such a contrast, one hand icy cold, the other burning. The theme of these meetings is family psychotherapy. Psycho means: the spirit. A subterranean spirit in the blood, a thought wrapped in flesh. Therapy means: care, caring for, healing. Family—you're not too sure. If you leave the word on its own in your thoughts, it conjures others: warmth, fusion, cocoon—suffocation. That's how you hear the theme of these meetings: caring for spirits that are suffocating. Healing souls that are being strangled. The morning begins and with it comes the buzzing of words behind the table. It is not a matter of indifference that between you and the words there is this table. The word is a perishable, ephemeral commodity. It takes on the color of the circumstances in which it is used. The same words uttered in different places are not the same words. The word of love can be said in passing, in the swing of a dancing step. It is light, and has no more than its lightness to express. The scholarly word is pronounced from behind a table. It is heavy with the wood of the table and the chair, and it is out of breath by the time it reaches you. The truth it contained has changed, in that lapse of time, into moralizing or ennui. Between these two extremes of words—love and reason, the open sky and the gray table—every combination, every intermediary is possible. For a long time nothing happens in the auditorium. Someone is reading notes into a microphone. Others copy down in their notebooks what is being read. Finally something happens: there comes a word that cannot be copied down, only heard. If this word draws our attention, it is because it is being staged. Two psychologists, a man and a woman, are describing in detail their encounters with a patient and his family. A young girl is suffering from hallucinations. She hears voices ordering her about, condemning her. In the course of their sessions, the questions asked of the parents cause the sad truth to emerge. In the beginning, a bit of mud, a bit of shame. A woman too full of life for the taste of those around her, a woman too free to submit to any law—except that of loving. The family wants nothing more to do with this woman. She doesn't belong there: banish her face and her name, erase her from all memory. The only place she may keep is in silence—an abscess of silence handed from one generation to the next, an affliction of silence swelling and bursting in this affliction of voices—in a child's suffering. The psychologists scrupulously relate the parents' words, pausing meaningfully before each of the most enlightening words. What surprises is not the story. It is actually quite banal. Every home has its hell. What surprises you is the pleasure of those telling the story, a contagious pleasure that spreads through the audience—the stain of pleasure oozing over the rows of the auditorium. The sick one is the woman who's talking and who doesn't know what she's saying. Doctors are people who think they know what is being said, and who are pleased to believe it. The sick one is the woman who is coming to the assistance of the doctors, helping the doctors take pleasure in the great relevance of their thoughts. The two psychologists talk in turn, sharing dialogues. As you listen you feel pleasure mingled with disgust. You see them as a couple. They use the same suave voice to say the most insidious things. The same jubilation in speaking. What makes a couple? What is it about the juxtaposition of a man and a woman that sometimes suggests this conjugal image? It does not necessarily mean that they have a shared history. Nor even that they necessarily share a lovers' understanding. Disagreement does not necessarily prevent the image of the couple from appearing. On the contrary. You listen to this story of two families—the doctors' version, and the patient's. What makes a couple is neither a bed nor a house nor a history. What makes a couple is what they eat together: a couple is two people breathing in the same air, swallowing the same food—the same bitterness or the same joy. And those two, what do they eat? They eat suffering, unhappiness. They delight in it, feast upon it. The words behind the table do not even reach you now. They stay on the table, and you look at the people picking them up with their hands to bring them to their lips, you look at the people so eager to be present at devouring entire portions of a dark truth, rotten words, and you are suddenly, violently nostalgic for another form of sustenance, you are seized by the desire to return to that light word beneath the corrugated metal roof—the exquisite savor of tea without water, childhood without remedies, the incurable truth, the perfection of tea without tea.

A Celebration in the Hills

5

She tells you: the house is in the hills, lost in the woods.
Follow me. Drive slowly because the road is bad. She's
ahead of you, alone in her car. And you're behind, in
another car. The road is a road in the south of France,
and the time is late at night. The sky is blue and black.
Ash made blue with stars crackling underneath, kin-
dled by an incensed, violent wind, a wind gone raving
mad. Before long you leave the road for a path that
climbs, a poor excuse for a path on close terms with the
stars. Finally the house, massive, closely guarded by
the dogs of the mad wind. You enter and immediately
encounter cool air and kindness. The cool air is that of

old stones, wooden stairs, rooms hollow and round like a belly, like a fable. The kindness is in words, the words of this young woman who has offered you asylum for the night. She tells you about herself, that is, about the people she loves. We are made of that, we are made of the people we love, nothing else. However reclusive our life might be, lost in hills seared with wind, it is never closer than in a cluster of beloved faces, in the thoughts that go out to them, in the breath that travels from them to us, from us to them. She speaks and you listen to the gravel of stars crunching in her voice. You are several hundred kilometers from home and yet you are there, in these loving words, quietly loving, gently loving; yes, you are in these words as if you were at home, in your own land. Your house is there—without stones or doors or windows, there, in the hills of words well worn by love, whitened by the wind of a pure love. You listen as you look at the walls, the objects and furnishings. You do not often leave home, and when you do you are prey to this astonishment—how others live, their concerns, their expectations, how they eat and what they die of, how they work and what they dream of, what they put in their houses and what they throw away, how they manage with life going by, day after day after day. The house this evening is simple, basic in appearance, you might say it's a house made for the wind, built for the comfort of the wind blowing through the stones and singing at the windows, lurking like a cat in the corridors. The young woman guesses what you are thinking. She says, you're right, it's a beautiful house. It found its true beauty on a summer evening like this, very long ago, in the next room. Death was there, in that room, and at the heart of death was my mother, already so old, so weary. A last effort and she was finally laid to rest, the rest about which we know nothing, except the fear it gives us, the rest in which hands are forever empty and the heart cracks open like a walnut between the teeth of a beast. That was my mother there, sleeping beneath life, yet it was no longer my mother, I don't really know how to explain. My mother was at the foundation of my heart—and suddenly the foundation gave way and my heart was falling with nothing to hold it back. I believed in God, vaguely, at the time. I believed the way you believe in springtime when you see the sweetness of a lilac bush or the delicacy of a certain light. But you know, you believe in God when things are going well, and when things are going badly you don't believe in anything anymore.

You're afraid; you're sick with fear. You look for a way out, you see, that's what it's about. You look for a way out, anything. There's no point making up stories, you know: nobody really believes in God. Even Christ had his face bathed in sweat as he prepared to die. You see, I know my Gospel: "My God, why hast thou forsaken me?" Go to hospitals, listen to war stories: they're not calling out to God, those soldiers in shreds on the battlefield. They're not asking for God, they're asking for their mother. And there I was with my heart in shreds and I couldn't call out to my mother. It would have been pointless to call out to her. Imagine: a motionless body, and all around, in ever larger waves, growing less and less silent, the light of a summer morning, the muffled voices of the adults (we were numerous that day, relatives and friends on vacation), and finally the laughter of little children running through the house as if they were in the depths of the forest, playing hide and seek, laughing as they hid in closets, shrieking when they were found. We let them do what they wanted. We didn't want the sadness of children—who could want such a thing, anyway. We simply said to them, there, the room is open, it's not a forbidden room. Grandmother has just died. She'll stay here for two days, then we'll put her in the earth. You can go and say good night to her. If you don't want to, it doesn't matter. We adults know a lot more than you do, but when we're faced with what's just happened we don't know any more than you do. The children listened closely to what we said. At first they didn't go into the room. We adults are afraid of death, almost as afraid of death as of life. And in the beginning the children took some of that fear upon themselves, some of that gravity which had suddenly come over us. They went around the house more slowly, almost calmly. But the fine vacation fever did not leave them. In the afternoon they went out the way they do every day. And it happened when they came back, splattered with laughter and games of tag. Seven or eight children, the eldest ten years old, the youngest four, their arms laden with wildflowers, cornflowers in particular, and there they go, bursting into the room, opening the shutters, and the little girl climbs onto the dead woman's bed, and the others hand her the cornflowers and they spread them out pell-mell, and they stay for a long time, one of them sitting cross-legged on the bed, another stretched out on the carpet. They stay for half an hour or an hour perhaps, talking about yesterday's games and the ones to come, then they leave the room, singing, a slight caress to the petrified face, and so it goes for two days:

thousands of footsteps from the fields and the wind to the bed, thousands of paths from the flowers and the sun to the sunken face on the white pillow. Even at night they went into the room, stifling their laughter so they wouldn't wake us. We were careful not to interfere. It was the only intelligent thing our sorrow had left us: above all, do not interfere. We were intimidated, yes, intimidated by the children's nobility, the basic nobility of their behavior, their manner — forgive me for speaking so clumsily — it was their way of staying close to God, the disheveled God of summer games played until the darkest of shadows. We let them invent this way of going into our sorrow, like starlings against a summer sky, like life into life. It lasted for two days. Two days and two nights. A celebration. A celebration the likes of which I'd never seen, one that did not diminish the tears, did not prevent the pain, but a real celebration all the same. And then on the second day something happened. It was the youngest girl who came to us. The children had left the table long before. We were enjoying the peace that comes at the end of a meal, the pleasure of speaking about serious things, miserably serious, frivolously serious — politics, work, you see what I mean — and the little girl came in, out of breath and radiant: quick, come quick, Grandmother is smiling. We followed her and saw for ourselves: in two days her face had changed. It had become simpler, there were almost no more wrinkles and, at the corners of her mouth was something like a smile. No, let me remove the "something like": a real smile, scarcely visible to be sure, but it's always like that, with invisible things. They're always on the faintest, frailest edge of the visible, scarcely perceptible, no taller than a child, never as tall as an adult, ever. Then the funeral was held, and a week later it was the end of vacation. This story dates from five years ago. Over the past five years this house has found its true beauty, its true place in the wind, under the stars. For five years now the wind has been at home here. Banished everywhere, and furious at being banished. It comes here to find peace and quiet, a resting place, a home. Ever since the day a tribe of children presided over the funeral of an old woman, in that same knowing way they have when they send a sparrow, found dead in the road, to heaven, with the grace which is theirs alone, which does not come from their surroundings or from anything known on earth, but where does it come from ... I've been wondering, and five years later I'm still wondering.

I hope my heart will hold up,
without craquelure

6

The tree is in front of the house, a giant in the autumn light. You are in the house near the window. You've got your back turned to it. You don't turn around to make sure it is still there—you never know with loved ones: you fail to look at them for a moment, and then the next moment they've disappeared or gone into the shadow. Even trees run away from time to time, or have their faithless moods. But you're sure of this one, sure of its illuminating presence. This tree has recently become one of your friends. You can tell who your friends are because they don't prevent you from being on your own, because they illuminate your solitude without interrupting it. Yes, that is how you can tell who your friends are: man, woman, or tree, like this one, gigantic and discreet. As discreet as it is gigantic. This tree is an inhabitant of the village where you sometimes spend a few days doing nothing, not even writing, above all not writing, in the village of Saint-Ondras in the Isère. Farther down the village, in front of another house, there is another tree, just as big, more chaotic as it reaches toward the sky, and you have an affair with that tree, too. A fir tree. You carry its photograph around in your wallet. It's the only picture you carry around with you. From time to time, in the slight sadness of a journey or an absence, people will show you a photograph from their wallet. Here, these are my kids, this is my wife. You only have this photograph of a fir tree to show. You don't show it, because of the words you would have to say. Here is a tree, it's not even mine. It's in a garden that doesn't belong to me. It's a tree and it's the clearest image of the person who took the photograph. She was washing the dishes in the kitchen and she raised her head and saw this tree through the tiny kitchen window. She took the picture at once and sent it on to me, a way of saying, this is what I saw today, at such and such a time, in such and such a riot of August light, in such and such a state of my heart, which by today has changed or stayed the same, this is the world, these are my eyes, at a particular hour of a particular day. This fir tree has been a friend for several years now. The other tree, the one from this morning, is a more recent acquaintance. The first time you saw it was last summer. You were drinking tea beneath its foliage. A cloud of shade in a cup of tea. Today is your second meeting, in autumn. It's cold. You are separated by a pane of glass. A pane of glass is not enough to keep you apart. The tree imparts a feeling of well-being, a sweetness in its presence that spreads through the house and has even entered the sleep you find there. You spent the night in this house. You're leaving again today. When you go down into the kitchen for breakfast, the two women who live here have already been up for a long time. They've already taken a walk in the surrounding countryside. They share another cup of coffee with you. On the wall opposite you is a painting by Bonnard. The painter's childhood home was not far from here, in Grand-Lemps. One of the young women is speaking. The clothes she is wearing are the same tones as the painting: muted colors, a smoldering light, colors of bygone summers, of lost love. Paradise's coat of arms: pink, lilac. Discussing painting is not like discussing literature. It's much more interesting. When you discuss painting you're quickly done with words, there's a rapid return to silence. A painter is someone who wipes the windowpane between the world and us with light, with a rag made of light, soaked in silence. A painter is someone constantly sending us photographs of the world. A multitude of pictures, too many pictures to squeeze them all into a wallet and take them out from time to time: here is the world the way it beats in the heart of a stranger. Here is the heart of a stranger beating in my heart. Bonnard died in 1947. The last entry in his last notebook said: "I hope my painting will last, without craquelure. I would like to appear before the young painters of the year 2000 upon butterfly's wings." His last painting was of an almond tree in bloom. A last breath, a last effort: go on, give it your all one last time, let everything flower at once, leave without regrets, without forgetting anything still deep within. There are two possible attitudes toward death. They are the same attitudes as toward life. You can flee into a career, an idea, plans. Or you can let things happen—pave the way, celebrate their passage. Death, about which we know nothing, will lay its hand upon our shoulder in the privacy of a room, or it will strike us in broad day-light—depending. Meanwhile the best we can do is facilitate its task, so that it will have almost nothing left to take, as we will have already given almost every-thing. So that all that death will hold in its fingers will be a few almond blossoms. An almond tree in bloom is very beautiful in the eyes of a dying person, and in their hands, and in their heart. It is almost as beautiful as a tall tree murmuring the simple life in Saint-Ondras, that holy place, in Isère. Now it is the second young woman who speaks. She tells a story that starts off fun-ny. She went to the doctor with a pain in her hand. He gave her some prescriptions, lots of prescriptions, and lots of injections into the ailing hand, several times a week. Months later he confessed to her that the injec-tions had served no purpose; they were just to make sure she would come back to him. There was nothing in the syringe—emptiness, absence. That is how love en-tered, by means of a trick, through the regularity of their encounters, her passion for him, and his for her: through regular injections of absence, injections of emptiness. How else could love enter? That is the way it came, that is the way it left again. Through emptiness, through absence. Through the doctor's growing fear, his fear of hurting his family, his image, God the father, everything and nothing. He hasn't been in touch for several weeks. She is suffering, a suffering with no conceivable remedy. There is a moment in art when the painter knows his painting is finished. He does not know why, he merely recognizes his sudden inability to change the slightest thing. The painting and the painter go their separate ways when they can no longer help each other. When the painting no longer knows how to nourish the painter, when the painter no longer knows how to nourish his painting. The work is complete when the artist, standing before his canvas, returns to his total solitude. Bonnard always delayed that moment. From his deathbed he asked a friend to make a change in the almond tree in bloom: there's a green that doesn't work, there, on the left; cover it over with a golden yellow. For another painting, on display in Paris, too far away, he wrote and asked that a green bird on the canvas be removed, covered over with brown paint. The woman speaking today stands before her love like the painter before his painting—reluctant to finish or make changes, trying to forestall the moment of solitude. Her words are not really meant for you, or for herself. They circle through the room and go outside to find refuge, in the tree gleaming with light—a little green bird, impossible to kill. Now you observe this woman with the attentiveness of a painter: her hands on the table, the silence in her eyes, the cry of all women in love: I hope my heart will hold out, without craquelure. I would like to appear before my lover of the year 2000 upon butterfly's wings.

It no longer frightens you

7

It no longer frightens you. It's still dangerous, unpredictable in its calmness. But the fear is gone, the fear is no longer part of its deepest, most impenetrable substance. The fear vanished in a second. Evaporated, dissolved, it left in the same way that lassitude can enter love: in an instant. In an instant and for all time. Until that day, there was fear between you. Fear was there like an unwritten law, sovereign in silence. All fears come from childhood, to chastise it, to prevent it from going its way. All children have an intimate, personal acquaintance with fear—but for a long time it does not affect them in their childhood. They circle around fear and brush up against it, and they might even play with it. You're afraid of insects and uniforms, of bad grades and dogs, you're afraid of ghosts. Fear is like adulthood making inroads into your childhood. It has a position, a time, it has a place. But it doesn't stop you. You fall down; you're afraid of falling and that makes you fall, then you get up again, you cry and then a second later you're laughing. Joy is still stronger. The joy of living for life's sake. Fear is night time, joy is day. Children deal with fear the way they deal with the night, with shadows, with their parents' inadequacies, the way they deal with everything. Fear is a material given in the world, among dozens of other such givens. You must understand that the black night accelerates the beating of the red heart. To be alone in sorrow or in the thick green foliage of a forest is terrifying. You must understand it, but it doesn't concern your spirit, what's inside you, it's just information about the world—like knowing that the north wind is icy, or that the snow always stays on the ground high in the mountains. So you learn things like this and then you forget, just as in childhood you immediately forget what you know in order to go out and play a bit farther down the road, to go on frittering away the hours, and to enjoy

the great happiness of frittering away the hours. It's
something parents have difficulty understanding, that
kind of pleasure. Don't just sit there doing nothing, do
something, pick up a book. They even want your games
to be educational — not just something for play, not
just something for nothing. That's because parents are
adults and adults are people who are afraid, who sub-
mit to their fear, who know it with a dark, servile
knowledge. Fear is no longer like it used to be in the
world, in certain places in the world, in the gilded mo-
ments of a legend or in the dark recesses of a street.
Now fear is in the mind of adults. In the blood of their
blood, at the heart of their hearts. It leads them from
one place to the next, it has at last got the better of in-
defatigable childhood. It makes marriages sad — for
fear of solitude. It leads to forced labor — for fear of
poverty. It makes lives absent — for fear of death.
When it slips over childhood, fear evaporates at once.
When it slips over adults, fear stays, accumulates. It's
like snow, a snow falling not onto the earth but onto
the spirit. The fear that enters an adult heart goes to
meet the fear that's already there. It collapses upon it-
self, it adds to itself like so much gray snow. So you stop
moving. So you forbid yourself from moving beneath

the dirty snow; you no longer leave your home, your marriage, your work, your worries. By clinging ever tighter to your life you hope to lessen the power of fear, to slow down the gray avalanche. You're like those animals that are suddenly petrified at the sound of the wind in the trees and become incapable of movement, unable to go any farther than themselves. How to escape such wretchedness? How to escape from a place one cannot remember entering? Childhood has neither beginning nor end. Childhood at the heart of everything. How can you reach the heart of everything? It happens whether you want it or not. It happens without you — through the grace of a love that is faster than you yourself, faster than your fear or the sound of the wind in the branches. Yes, that is how you finally managed to go back to it after such a long period of waiting, of fear. All at once. From one day to the next. And now you can longer do without it. Someone says to you: you know, you shouldn't go out so far, it can kill all the same. But you no longer believe that, or rather you answer: it can do what it likes with me. The enjoyment is too great for me to leave it. How could I have spent so many summers without it? So many white or blue hours so distant from it ... To be sure, there were books. Reading is what resembles it the most. You actually go toward it with a handful of books—that you will not open. It fills you with delight, so much more delight than any of the finest books. That summer you go down every day, in the late afternoon. You think, good, I'm going for a swim. But it would be more exact to say: excuse me, I have an appointment, a date with the water; before I was afraid of it, now I want nothing else; it's like a love affair, you see, maybe even better than a love affair, yes, clearly better. There are several paths you can take to your tryst. You can follow the shade-filled canal or cross the countryside furrowed with light. However you get there, you will find happiness: the vastness of the pond, there, so close by. Long and narrow and surrounded by trees. It's not even such wonderful water; sometimes it's a bit earthy. You go in without wariness, you go right to the heart of it, right to the middle, at an equal distance from either shore. Your face lifted slightly to the sky, your body gliding through the water as through a light silk. There is no longer any fear. Fear departed with the thought of it. That thought is no longer in your mind. It is no longer inside but out: you go into the water the way you go into a thought that could think itself all on its own, without you. You swim for a long time in this external thought, in the water of the world. For a long time, your mind empty, your body weightless. When you come out of the water, it's not to leave it behind but to contemplate it all the better, from farther away, with the peaceful gaze that follows love. To see the way it catches the light, how it changes with the imperceptible movement of the hours, how it reacts to the most secret moods of the sky. You knew this pond when you were a child. Then you forgot about it. From then on you had a problem with summer: you never knew what to do with it. You were faced with summer, or vacation, the way one is faced with marriage or work: you know how it works, but you don't know what purpose it serves. Now you know: summer serves no purpose—like love, or joy. You no longer find the time to read, to write, to answer invitations. You can't think of anything but the water. When it's there you are lost in it. When it's no longer there you wait for the moment when you'll see it again. It's something like a love story, except there is no story. But love really is there. It has no shape, no face, no name. But it really is there. It came the way all love comes, after the end of time—the end of death, the end of fear.

8

It could be the story of two lights. Two material lights—the yellow light of bulbs and the white of a neon tube. It's night all around, nothing but darkness. Material night: bodies tucked in bed, cars in their parking spaces, animals in the forest. Yes, you could begin the story like that, or you could begin it with the end: the confusion of two lights, separate in space, separate in time, each igniting the same part of your mind. And the first light to begin with, the neon. It's already several years old. It returns every year in late autumn and lasts until March. For years the same buzzing neon, the same milky white light wrenching the same bay window from the darkness at night, with the same figure standing in the middle of the window. You go by with the children or on your own, past the center for mentally handicapped people. A group of low buildings scattered at the end of a green lawn. By day what surprises you most is the green, the close-cut grass thirsting from drought, filling your eyes with despair. Green water, thin with boredom. An expanse of hopelessness, flattened and crushed, a web of green resignation. The grass is always the same height. It never ventures toward lushness, toward the carefree folly of kindergartens. Nor does it ever die or languish into blackened patches. There must be a gardener looking after it. They must have arranged for a gardener to look after the ailing grass, just as there are those who look after the handicapped people. Nothing must be either too dry or too high. Nothing must die and nothing must live. People on the outside often say: such dedication; how hard it must be to look after people like that; if I were in your place ... You could say the same thing to the gardener: how hard it must be to look after that grass; such a uniform green; such a hopelessly green green; such dedication, such rectitude amid boredom, such loyalty amid lassitude. If I were in your place ... But there's something else to be said about that green. Yes, you could say: this green expanse, you've already seen it somewhere. The same thing. The same green melancholy, the same color of loneliness, surrounding private homes. A tiny little yard of green around families. When the good weather returns, the inferno of lawnmowers begins. The husband heroically mows the lawn, he's pleased with himself, proud to contribute to familial duty, to transform the dissatisfaction of a week of work into a blaring noise. The color green, in painting, is obtained by mixing blue and yellow. The green of lawns is not a mixture of blue and yellow, but of gray and black. The gray of a week of work, the black of the Sunday that is never Sunday, nothing but the day before another week of work. And there's more. There's more to say about this green: this domesticated green, this green enclosure, it's something you also find in front of big middle-class houses, behind the fences of private villas. There is a lot of lawn, too, an enormous quantity of well-behaved green. Around the mental poverty and the financial power. Wherever spirit is lacking and money abundant: lawns. Clear green lawns entrusted to the competent hands of gardeners. On winter evenings, when you go by the center for the mentally handicapped, you can't see the lawn. It is resting in the darkness. It has returned to its original darkness. It has finished its work, which is to leave your vision helpless, the better to dissuade you from entering or taking a single step onto that green desolation, for fear that you might want to go and take a closer look at those people crippled in their mind, or at those sleeping on their money. At night you can't see the center, only the bay window opposite the entrance, and the man standing in the shower of light, beneath the pallor of the neon. He stays there for hours. A big man in his pajamas, his arms folded over his chest. He stands facing outward, for hours, after dinner—which is always served very early in such places, like in hospitals all around the world, to make things easier for the personnel. Between meal time and bed time a dark expanse, a large lawn of time. There, between eating and sleeping, in the electric light, a man stands, in his pajamas. He rocks from one foot to the other, for hours on end. A fat man behind the bay window, a silhouette of black paper against a milky background. An enormous child holding himself in his arms, giving himself the lullaby he needs to go to the repast of sleep, the necessary courage to go from this minute to the next. That's

all. After the nasty green of the grass, that's all you can
see of the center for the handicapped: this swaying
from one foot to the other beneath the moon of a neon
light. Years go by. The image comes back to you. It's
like an appointment: the fat man in pajamas and the
swaying of his body, from the right foot to the left. For
hours. Hours, autumns, winters. Finally one day you go
into the center. You gain access in the best possible
way: without notice, without warning. You go in
through the voice of the woman speaking to you. This
woman speaking to you is going to pieces. She works at
the center. She is not going to pieces because of her
work. She doesn't tell you much about it, just that the
mentally handicapped can sometimes be nasty, and
her words reassure you, as if reducing the strangeness
of the patients to a slight difference within human-
kind—within it, not on the outside. As if the ability to
be nasty were a sign of belonging to the same commu-
nity, the same world. But she's tired of talking about
her work. It's not the hours she's spent in those build-
ings eroded by green that have reduced her to pieces,
to dust, to ash. It's merely a love story, a story you listen
to without interrupting, a story to do with the other
source of light—the bulbs. The woman talking to you

is married, she has children. You see the children, but not the husband. This is an affliction you have, something wrong with your eyesight: you never see the couple in a couple. You never manage to see as far as two. You see one plus one, never the combination of the two. You have a childish aversion to any kind of society — and society begins with two, with disastrous speech of this type: my husband and I, we think that; my wife and I, we are in the habit of. It's mainly women who want marriage. They want it with an absolute, insane will. The man submits to it, or so it seems. He enters into marriage the way one enters into a new profession. He learns its rules the way a child learns its lessons, complaining. Because he doesn't expect much from marriage, the man does not despair of it and won't want to get out of it, even in the case of bankruptcy — just the way you stick with a job that no longer gives you any pleasure, but that helps make ends meet. For women, it's different. Men are like everybody, women are like no one. This woman speaking to you — her story is simple, on the surface. It's the story of her passion for someone. They work together at the center for the handicapped. For months nothing happened. Then one day it was everything. Why that day, why not the day before or the day after, or never, that's inexplicable. Nor does she seek to explain it. Rapture contains its own intelligence. The darkness of pleasure penetrates all light. In the beginning she lies about her work schedule. She comes home later and later. She spends part of the night with the other man. Then she talks to her husband. She tells him what is going on—the speed of an event she no longer has any control over. She is thinking of leaving, of divorce. The invisible story begins there. Invisible, beneath an open sky. The husband says nothing, does absolutely nothing. No tears, no lamentation. Neither the affliction of insults nor that of melancholy. Every night he turns on every light in the house. He waits. He waits in the brightly-lit house. She comes back in the middle of the night. She comes into the bedroom, lies down beside him and weeps—for a long time, silently. The story goes on for a century and then comes to an end. The other man leaves her. He leaves her but he is still there. They are still in the same building circled with green, still looking after the same people at the same time, every day. Salaried work was invented so you would not think about what makes you suffer, so every day those same hours would come when you weren't thinking about yourself, or solitude, or God, or others, so you would not think about all that you suspect might be insoluble, heart-wrenching. And now there's no way out. The passion is still there. It has turned to hatred but it is still there, intact. She says this with a smile: there's no place for me anymore. Neither there at the center, not here in this house. There I've lost everything, here I'm given everything. But it's something else that I want—something else besides a husband or a lover. In love stories there are only stories, never love. If I look around, what do I see: people who are dead or wounded. Couples who retire at the age of thirty or couples who make a career of suffering. I'm not interested in any of that—in falling asleep at home or insomnia outside. What am I waiting for—I don't know. Maybe nothing. It's very hard to obtain, nothing. When you're a child they make you a promise. The promise is life. So why don't they keep it, so why do I still keep hoping they'll keep it, that promise? I'll never become resigned, I'll never retire. I no longer go out at night but that doesn't mean I've come home. My husband knows that. He keeps waiting, he keeps using up electricity with the lights. Nobody has helped me the way he has. But what can kindness do against despair. She tells you once again how weary she feels, tired of herself and of everything. She evokes death, a departure or a new love the way you might talk about your upcoming vacation abroad, hesitating over which resort. Finally she laughs at herself, gets up, and puts on a record, a Vivaldi concerto. You listen with her to how the sound crackles, the dust of fluid song. This music goes with the night over the town and into the soul, a music rendering the night soft and deep, a purple night where only two lights are lit, in a building in the center, in a house in town, two images blending together, a single light in all the dark expanse, the blaze of an impossible life and this remedy that could extinguish the blaze, a single gesture: swaying from one foot to the other, the monotonous sweetness like a gift to oneself, enveloping oneself, a lullaby that one anguished heart sings to another.

Mina

9

You had already written a piece about her. You'd shown it to her and then thrown it out. All wrong. The portrait was all wrong, and there was nothing to salvage. You wanted so badly to write that text, and you can't force things where writing is concerned, any more than you can with love. You can't say, "I would like to love you." You say, "I love you," and as you say it you discover a much deeper love than any willing of it. They taught you things in school. In your family, too. But the important things, you had to learn them for yourself, by stuttering, stumbling, this thing for example: the wretchedness of a will that has only itself to rely upon, the madness of a life built like a fortress. You've always avoided people who have their certainty and their will, those principled people strangled by the laces of their life. In the time it took to write that other text, you became like them, you became a professional writer, someone who knows how to do things and who, no longer believing in anything but that knowledge, no longer allows the mystery of things to enter his heart—those very things that resist the control of one's will. Professionalism is a disease people contract through their job, through their mastery of it, and it enslaves them. You wanted to create a portrait of her because you wanted to capture a bit of her light, and because you know of no other reason to write: every presence has its singular grace, just waiting to be told. Now that your impatience has left you, you can take up the abandoned portrait. Now that the canvas is blank, you can return to it, like the painter to his task. What she has just told you in the space of ten seconds should suffice: the rest was wrong—visible, certainly, and yet wrong because it had no bearing upon her life. For something to be true it must, in addition to being true, enter into our life. Everything she experienced, however, took place in her absence, far from her. This happens quite often:

you can remain single through ten years of marriage. You can talk for hours without saying a thing. You can sleep with the whole world and remain a virgin. There had been a period of her life, six months, a year, where she had slept with the whole world and that period, like the others, had no bearing upon her life. She had men come to her house, or she went to theirs. Before getting undressed she would ask for money. She talks about it as if it were some temp job, as if she were subbing: it taught me nothing about men or about myself. What it taught me was something I already knew. It didn't exist for six months, a year, for nothing. And she bursts out laughing. There you have it, one good thing accomplished: everything has been wiped clean, erased, from the first painting, that first text, now you can write the second one with the chance knowledge of those ten seconds yesterday on the telephone, uttered in passing, "My first doll was called Mina." You don't know who Mina was, so she explains: it's the name of Dracula's fiancée. When she was five she gave the name to her doll, after her father had told her the story about Dracula, who kills by night and sleeps by day, the story of the great professional of the darkness who was not allowed to die but who could not live. And she adds: my father told me all the books—fables, Homer, Shakespeare, the whole lot of them. Adults, when they talk to a child, force their voice. They remove what is obscure and secret from their words. They talk about wolves and storms, ogres and springs, but they are silent about the rest: self-interest, lies, weariness. The powerful urge toward murder, deep in one's soul, and the even more powerful hope for a pure love. My father knew that I knew everything. The heart grows slowly. The mind is at its sharpest right at the start. The heart takes a long time. The mind is immediately in full flower. Even if one must act extremely gently with children, one can entrust them with everything, even the things one does not know how to say. In the evening my father would come to the edge of my fatigue, and he would sit by the side of my bed and tell me the story of the world: Red Riding Hood and Dracula, Ulysses and Ophelia, Hamlet and Cinderella, Don Quixote and Snow White. Every evening a book, even before I knew how to read. What she has told you now illuminates and composes the portrait you had failed to see: her childhood in Bordeaux, a majestic and funerary city, her arrival in Paris, her first marriage then her second, prostitution and encounters with the most brilliant minds in the capital, everything passing by her as if in a dream, until the discovery of a cancer buried in her breast like a treasure. Until that recent day nothing had been able to touch the clarity of the early years, the smoldering fire of the beloved voice upon a five-year-old's heart: "Close your eyes, Mina, don't say another thing. Listen to the sound of galloping in your heart. It's a proud little horse who never tires, and on his back a messenger is riding. You're the one he left at dawn and you're the one he's riding back to. Listen Mina to the wind whipping his coat around him and reddening his white hands; listen to the thundering of red light, Hamlet and his skull, Bluebeard and his keys, Ulysses and his bow; listen to how life is not allowed to live, to what mortal sweetness there is in dreams. Take care of yourself, Mina dear, take care of yourself." In the meantime the girl of five was growing and continued to seek for gold in the talk of intellectuals, or on the faces of men made stupid by something as weak as the sight of a naked woman. What is it we love in those we love? We believe we love them for themselves, but what is that exactly, "themselves?" Where does the person cease — her contours, her limits, and where does that part of her that is so much more than who she seems begin — the pain in her voice, the innocence in her eyes? The grace you recognized in this woman came from the love given to her at the age of five — the way one can detect in the beauty of flowers the glittering of the rains that scolded them. Forty years have passed since then. Forty and five make forty-five. At the center of the portrait is a forty-five year old woman. In the background and to the right is a little ash-heap of husbands, lovers, and books. In her arms there is a doll. In the doll's mouth is an unpronounceable word. My name is Ophelia. I'm forty-five years old now. I'm recovering from cancer. The doctors were very kind to me. They took away my clothes, my hair and my sweet-water smile. They assured me I'd get all my things back soon. I don't know if they're telling the truth. Doctors are like adults when they speak to children; they talk to you so that you don't hear, so in the end you hear too much. My name is Snow White. I'm forty-five years old now. For a long time I was lost in the depths of the world. Those who loved me made me invisible and light, far too light to be happy. My name is Cinderella. I'm forty-five years old now. My stomach is upset from having eaten all sorts of food. No one ever taught me to separate sweet and salty, flesh from soul, life from dreams. The men who shared my meals got off better. Men always get off better; perhaps they just nibble at life. My name is Mina, I'm forty-five years old now. I was born in Bordeaux and I died in Paris. I feel better now. I'm resting and gradually rediscovering the world. My father is not here anymore to tell me stories but I'll manage on my own. I've understood what's most important. There are the things people tell you and there is the way they tell you, and it's the way that makes all the difference. It's the only thing that matters. People who have said to me "I love you" didn't know what they were saying and they said it badly. In my bedroom when I was a child, there was Shakespeare, and there was my father. Shakespeare who said that life was a tale full of sound and fury told by an idiot, and my father who was reading Shakespeare to me, and I wasn't listening to the story, I was listening to his voice, the triumph of his voice in the capital of my heart. His voice rang true. The wordless voice told the truth about living, the voice of a sweet nocturnal love. Medicine has burned the tissues of my breast and all the books in my library, but it is powerless against that clear confident voice. That's where I am now and where I'll stay. I'll stay with that love given once and for all to a little girl's heart. I don't read nearly as many books but that doesn't matter: I understand where they come from. I understand the tiny grain of truth they contain. Fables tell the truth about love; I understand what they're saying. It all fits in a single sentence, and if I were a philosopher I would formulate it like this: what saves us does not protect us from anything, and yet it saves us. But because I've never looked for the truth as a philosopher, rather as a musician, because from the age of five I've given my attention to the timbre of the voice more than to the words raised up by that voice, I will say the sentence like this, that same sentence: take care of yourself, my little girl, take care of yourself, love.

I got up in the middle
of the meal

10

She calls at nine in the evening. You hesitate for a mo-
ment before answering: you're still afraid of the tele-
phone, still haunted by the idea of being invaded.
There's nothing to be said on the phone. Nothing to be
heard, only a crackling sound—or else the news of an
accident, or sorrow. The phone lines render only the
most banal things, or tragedy; endless chatter, or sud-
den death. Between the two there is nothing. One day
someone to whom you confessed your distaste for such
deafening communication answered you with a smile:
what on earth do you mean, how naïve, what an utter
lack of common sense. Look at what goes on in industry:

nothing can be decided without the telephone. It would be senseless to try to write letters to deal with matters. Look around you, for heaven's sake: no more horses on the roads, no more messengers running to the city with a parchment rolled up under their cloak. You listen, smile in turn, say nothing. You've never been any good at quick-witted replies, and only a week after this conversation do you come up with the right answer: you might be able to negotiate a contract, give news or place an order over the telephone, but there is at least one thing that is not possible, and for you that impossible thing is the only indispensable thing in life, and the most essential: a love letter. You cannot write a love letter over the telephone. It's not that the voice is not enough; on the contrary, the voice is too much. You can only speak properly of love from a great distance, where breath, where everything is lacking. Yesteryear people knew that, yesteryear in the twelfth century. They knew it by heart when they chanted *love from afar*, the queen absent. Distance brings sweetness. Absence tames what is near. Nowadays women still know this, as they speak of love to their shadow, to their mirror or to their dress—never to the one for whom all these lights, all these fields of wild grass cut in his absence, are blazing. The loving word is a vanished word. It can neither be said nor heard, and if it is, then it's not love dancing but love reasoning, love as a business contract, a simple crackling, a hackneyed thing somewhere between chatting and dying. No, there is no way to speak on the telephone—unless it's the way she spoke that evening, stuttering, hesitating, holding back her tears between each word. She often calls you, to talk about a book or a child. She is raising children of all ages, she devours things written under every sky. Many books of German poetry. She has translated a few of them, bringing them, out of love, as close to her voice as she can, into the cradle of her breath, into the domain of a native tongue. This evening she doesn't want to talk to you about books but about someone who makes books, a writer, that particular type of writer known as a philosopher. The passion for ideas is a childish passion, an angry one. Philosophers are like small children, expressing the power of their desire by assembling colored blocks as big as their hands. They pile and build and then knock the whole thing over with a wave of their hand. Me first, shouts the two-year-old, raising the wall of his cubes. I am everywhere, murmurs the thinker, raising his delight in formulas to the sky. But she is telling you about a philosopher who has just died and no longer says that sort of thing, and he hadn't been saying that sort of thing for a long time, not since the night he strangled his wife with his long fingers, the same fingers with which he would touch a white page or open a precious tome. You're familiar with this story. It touched the surface of the newspapers, a few lines about a brilliant intellectual, one of the stars of his generation—and then this sudden eclipse, a night stripped of stars. The medical profession had stepped in before the law: severe depression, irresponsibility. Ten years went by. Ten years locked away in a hospital then in a retirement home, and silence everywhere, bars of silence against the windows. In newspapers the world is an orderly place. The page with the sensational items is the graveyard of the poor. You rarely see an intellectual in there. An intellectual is never poor, even when he has no money. You can tell the rich by the cut of their clothes. You can tell the intellectual by the fall of his words. Words, like money, make for affluence. Words, more than money, make for affluence. Those who possess words possess the world. Look at poor people's clothes. Look at their shoes, look at their houses. Look as long as you like, you'll never know a thing about poverty until you have seen the face of a poor person confronted by those who know, who decide and judge. Poor people hear nothing of what their masters are saying to them; they simply intuit that those self-assured words are stealing the world from them, that such elegant speech and the injustices they suffer somehow go hand in glove. It is not knowledge that is at stake — it is the morbid splendor of a language that cares about itself and itself alone, the horror of a language that makes its own way into its affluence, leaving life behind in its wake. That manner of talking without ever taking any risks was something that kings had taken to the extreme, speaking of themselves only in the first person plural: we have decided. We have decreed. This senseless distance between a person and what he or she is saying is the source of all ascendancy over the world and ruination of the soul. You had already encountered philosophers and you had often perceived the abyss that exists between their opulent speech and the poverty of their life behind that speech, a life deprived of air. What astonished you when you read the newspaper was not so much the news of the philosopher's collapse as the discovery of how violent his ruin was: a spring wound tight for so long that suddenly it gave way, crushing books, thought, life. It's the rest of the story that your friend is telling you this evening on the telephone — the years of abandonment, the embarrassment of colleagues, how friends deserted him, how mourning became impossible. She met him several times in his wilderness. One day he came to eat at her house. He was calm, very calm, his face dark as ink, his eyes shadowed with rain and a gentleness in his voice — the immense gentleness of someone who would have preferred punishment to melancholy, a prison cell to tranquillizers, the immense gentleness of someone who devoured his death and his life all at once. She says: I watched him eat. I observed those fine hands that had brought death. I got up in the middle of the meal, went out into the garden and cut a rose to give to him, to place in those hands. And it's the same every time, you know how it is: it is not the one giving, but the one receiving, who makes the greatest offering. It was a yellow rose. He took it with him, to his little room with its bed, its sink, its table. Months later the rose was still there, a cold light in a glass. Toward the end he had no more visits, no more letters — nothing except that petrified flower in the room, a mummy of light. Why does one write books? Why does one use one's strength and time to write book after book, to make a career in ideas or beauty? Why does one take time from sleep, from love, from everything just to write a book, yet another book? Philosophers say: for clarity. Poets say: for gentleness. But however quickly they reply, they are too late for the reply that has always been there, has always been given, everywhere: to be loved. For the glory of being loved. This answer is one you have always heard. It is as valid for books as for everything else, and that might be why we do everything we do—money, children, or books: so that money, children, and books will bring you the love that is lacking. Parents beg their children for the strength to live. Writers demand with their inky voices for the kiss of illumination. Yes, you've always known that reply, and it has always seemed false to you, or its truth has seemed shaky, good for bad parents, good for bad writers. There's nothing you can do to be loved—or else it is only bad things, bad books, incomplete children. Love cannot be measured by what you do. Love comes without reason, without measure, and leaves again in the same way. When it is there, there is nothing more you can do. In its absence you can write, if you want; write. With a bit of luck the writing will touch on the truth. That truth will stay fresh within the book, and the book will be put away alongside the others. And that's it, and it's pointless, and everyone knows books are pointless, writing is the same as not writing, nothing else matters except that flower, picked after the end of the world, that yellow rose in those long hands, a true word of love, at last a true thought, at last the right word, offered in silence, received in silence—a withered rose in a tooth glass, a light flickering right up to the end in the little room with the bed, the sink, the table.

I am just back from Brittany, my love. Brittany is a land as beautiful as childhood, a place where fairies and devils get on well together. There are stones, water, the sky, the faces — and your name everywhere, singing beneath the name of stones, water, sky and faces.

It's been a long time now that I never go out without you. I take you along in the simplest of hiding places: I hide you in my joy like a letter in the midday sun.

In Brittany there are many churches, almost as many

churches as there are springs or devils. In one chapel I saw a boat as wide as two outspread arms. It had neither sails nor mast—only candles. It was like a child's toy. On the hull its name was painted in blue: *Abandoned to the will of God*. I immediately thought of you: this little boat is your life and it is you, my love. It is the purity of your heart shipwrecked a thousand times over, a thousand times over heading back out to sea, taking with it the light that burns and cleanses it.

I cannot get enough of purity. I cannot get enough of that purity which has nothing to do with morality, but which is life in its elementary atom, the simple, stripped-down fact that we are all on the edge of the waters of our dark death, waiting there alone, infinitely alone, eternally alone. Purity is the most common matter on earth. It is like a dog: each time we rest upon nothing but our empty heart, purity comes to sit at our feet and keep us company.

That is something you taught me, my soul. You have taught me many things. At first you locked me in your laughter like a schoolboy in a classroom in the month of August, then you gave me back to the world, and my homework was to write the world as it is: terribly dark on the surface, miraculously pure underneath.

In the train that took me to Brittany, I read a book by Catherine of Siena. A fourteenth-century saint. I don't know much about her, except that she was in the habit of reminding the popes and the powerful of their own truth, with that violence women have when defending their children. The child of a saint is mad love, love driven mad from knowing nothing other than one's own self in a world that is nothing.

The movement of the train was taking me away from you, and the movement of my reading was taking me closer: the saints resemble you in their cheerful disorientation and the way they would throw their heart out the first open window. Saints are the most beautiful of women. They are beautiful with the strength that leaves them. In their voices I find the same silence as in the testimonies of survivors from concentration camps—as if suffering and love, in their extremes, cling to the same taciturn nerve. A woman whose head has been shaved and a saint whose heart has been burned both know what it is to have lost their voice. We will tell you our story, say those who were deported, but the more we tell you, the less you will understand, and you will never be able to hear what we will never know how to say. We call, say the saints, we call those who wait on the far shore of our heart, and we shall never know if they hear us, or even if there is anyone there. Both cases have to do with the exhaustion of language, for they touch on what is weakest in life, when life is nothing but pure joy or pure pain, the anonymous wasting away from hunger, the indefinite languor of absence: the ordeal of life at its weakest is the most radical ordeal there is.

That is one of the things I learned while looking at you. I could spend my life watching you live: one never wearies of the spectacle of intelligence. Your gestures, as you wipe a child's lips, or turn the pages of a book that you won't have the time to read; the way you complete a task where you barter your solitude for a pittance — everything in you offers a profound lesson. If I want to know the meaning of courage, or the nobility of existence, I have only to look at you and write down what I see.

I have been writing since you have been reading me, since that first letter, the one where I did not know what

I could possibly say, a letter that could only find its meaning in your eyes. I have never written anything more than the first three sentences of that letter: *To believe nothing. To expect nothing. To hope that something, some day, might happen.* Words lag behind our lives. You have always been ahead of what I hoped for from you. You have always been someone I never dared hope for.

In Brittany I looked at the faces, the waves, and the skies, and never have I been so aware of the sweetness of this life promised to death: we should enlighten each presence with a love that, each time, is unique, destined to its inconsolable and pure solitude. We should learn to count, one by one, each face, each wave, and each sky, in giving to each one the light it deserves in this darkened life.

All that is wrong with life comes from a lack of care for what is frail and ephemeral in it. Evil has no other cause than our negligence, and goodness can be born only of a resistance to our tendency to fall asleep, of an insomnia of the spirit that will raise our attentiveness to a point of incandescence—even if such pure attentiveness is basically impossible: only a God could take part in naked life without ever failing, without his presence ever lapsing into sleep, into thought, into desire. Only a God could care so little about himself to care, *relentlessly*, about the life that is marvelously lost with each passing instant. God is the name of that place which is never darkened by a negligent act, the name of a lighthouse on the shore. And perhaps that place is empty, and perhaps that lighthouse has always been abandoned, but it really doesn't matter at all: we have to act as if the lighthouse were kept, as if the lighthouse were inhabited. We have to come to God's help there on his rock and call, one by one, to every face, every wave, every sky—without forgetting a single one.

What I'm telling you now comes from you. I've learned, through observing your simple life, what women know through the pain of knowing, through the necessity of pain and place, and what men are so slow to hear, entrenched in their male complacency, their mastery of the world's appearances, its appearances alone: the closer one comes to the frail delicacy of life, the closer one approaches pure goodness, without the hope of one day ever reaching it: no one is holy in this life, which holy women know only too well, for they know what they are, the most lost among women—measuring through the range of a chant the magnitude of their loss. No one is holy in this life, only life itself is that.

My heart travels as poorly as a basket of strawberries, but in Brittany I never failed to relish the singing lightness of the days — another name for purity, another name for you, my love.

You are present wherever I go, and I see the world through your clear eyes: it is like a wooden footbridge between the two of us, a bridge we have always crossed.

You were there, your entire self, in the simple sensation of the breeze on my cheeks as I walked along the shore: it's hard to explain this and I'm not sure there's any need to explain what one lives. Life is its own meaning, provided it is living.

This voyage lasted just four days, yet it seems to me I could go on telling you about it for years. Very little gives me much to see. *Very-little* is for me the name for abundance. In my heart there's a wild animal that only comes out at night and only for a few seconds. It grabs the leftovers abandoned by the day — a leaf, a face, a word—and hurries back to its lair, and now it has enough to eat for two centuries. It never feeds off the same thing twice—here a trip, there a book, elsewhere silence; it is always the same joy sought, sometimes found—a childish joy, delicate as a patch of sunlight.

I don't believe I could ever lose you unless I lost that tiny grain of joy one needs to breathe, simply breathe. And it does happen to me, of course. Why shouldn't it happen to me? To describe this state to you, I would have to speak of it like an illness: the temperature of my dreams drops by several degrees. The pulse of my spirit grows fainter. Thoughts vanish. All that remains is that life on the surface which has never been a life for anyone. It is like a viral contamination of the spirit, a lack of faith, not in God, not even in myself—just a lack of faith, the way one speaks of a lack of sugar or red blood cells.

In such moments the love of life is injured. It is always the love within that is injured, and it is always from love that we suffer, even when we think we're not suffering.

As a small child I would sulk in the contemplation of a bedroom ceiling or the edge of the sidewalk, and that showed me more of hell than all the wise books I would read later. Hell is life when we no longer love it. A life without love is a life abandoned, far more abandoned than a dead man.

But even in such moments I don't lose you altogether: you are, my love, the joy that remains when I have no more joy.

One day I will tell you how much I forget you in the first face I see, and how much I find you there again.

There's a smile on my face as I write this letter and, no doubt, I have been writing it solely for the sake of that smile, a smile you give me. I still have many things to say to you. I'll put them into books: I have never written for anyone but you, in the hope that the idiocy of love will rescue me from the stupidity of literature.

Go on then, little boat, go on, tossed upon the waves, go to deliver your cargo of light.

I send you kisses.